Who-doku

Sudoku with Personality

Roy Leban

STERLING

New York / London
www.sterlingpublishing.com

For my wife, Emily Dietrich,
my chief puzzle tester

STERLING and the distinctive Sterling logo are registered trademarks of
Sterling Publishing Co., Inc.

2   4   6   8   10   9   7   5   3   1

Published by Sterling Publishing Co., Inc.
387 Park Avenue South, New York, NY 10016
© 2008 by Roy Leban
Distributed in Canada by Sterling Publishing
C/o Canadian Manda Group, 165 Dufferin Street
Toronto, Ontario, Canada M6K 3H6
Distributed in the United Kingdom by GMC Distribution Services
Castle Place, 166 High Street, Lewes, East Sussex, England BN7 1XU
Distributed in Australia by Capricorn Link (Australia) Pty. Ltd.
P.O. Box 704, Windsor, NSW 2756, Australia

Manufactured in the United States of America

Sterling ISBN-13: 978-1-4027-4948-3
ISBN-10: 1-4027-4948-1

For information about custom editions, special sales, premium and
corporate purchases, please contact Sterling Special Sales
Department at 800-805-5489 or specialsales@sterlingpublishing.com.

CONTENTS

His novel _ _ _ _ _ _ _ was the
first he wrote and the last one published.

| M | A | R | K | I | N | F | E | Z |

E		R	K			A	F	
	○		M	F		E		
Z		○						
K	I		○					
M			F	○	N			I
					○		M	E
						○		R
		I		N	E		○	
	M	E			K	I		Z

_ _ _ _ _

_ _ _ _ _

4

INTRODUCTION

Sudoku puzzles are all fine and good, but I've always been a bit disappointed that there was no "final answer" to the puzzle—no theme as in crosswords—nothing to give me that satisfying "I got it!" That's why I invented Who-doku puzzles. In addition to being a complete sudoku puzzle using nine distinct letters, each puzzle contains an internal clue to a final answer, which is revealed as the puzzle is completed.

If you're already familiar with sudoku puzzles, the extra rules for Who-doku puzzles are simple (see page 4 for a sample puzzle):

Use the letters at the top instead of the numbers 1 through 9.

The circled cells complete the clue for the final answer. Fill these in at the top of the page.

The shaded cells provide the final answer. Enter these letters on the lines below the corresponding column. When a column has more than one shaded cell, you'll have to determine which letter goes in which row of the final answer.

And, if you're not already familiar with sudoku puzzles or want a refresher, read on.

Sudoku is a type of logic puzzle whose appeal lies in its simplicity coupled with its addictiveness. While normal sudoku puzzles use numbers, Who-doku puzzles use letters. Each puzzle consists of a 9×9 grid of cells that is divided into nine smaller 3×3 sections called boxes. Some of the cells already contain letters and it is your task to fill in the rest of the cells with letters following a few simple rules:

Each row contains all 9 letters of the puzzle.

Each column contains all 9 letters of the puzzle.

Each 3×3 heavily outlined box contains all 9 letters of the puzzle.

This is accomplished using logic only, so that you never have to guess blindly. Each puzzle has a unique solution; that is, with the letters given, there is only one possible solution that will work. Harder puzzles require more advanced logic steps, as well as a bit more patience.

Each Who-doku puzzle also has a final answer that is a well-known person. As you're solving the puzzle, the circled cells will complete the clue at the top of the page, while the shaded cells will complete the person's name at the bottom of the page. You can wait until you're done with the puzzle to look at the circled and shaded letters or you can fill them in as you're going. Or, if you're stuck on sudoku logic and need some help, you can guess at the clue words or the name as a way to fill in extra cells. Although guessing the clue or answer is never required, you may find it useful with the more difficult puzzles at the end of the book.

When solving a sudoku puzzle, it is common to repeat the numbers from 1 to 9 to yourself over and over as you look for what numbers are missing. In this book, the nine letters are arranged in a phrase that is easy to remember, such as "MARK IN FEZ" in the example puzzle on page 4. You'll probably find yourself repeating the phrase or the letters in it to yourself while solving, as an easy way of checking the letters.

Look at the second cell in the top row of the example puzzle. By examining the other letters in the top row, we know that this cell cannot contain any of the letters E, R, K, A, and F. And by examining the other letters in the second column, we can eliminate I and M, leaving only N and Z. But the box already contains a Z, so we can deduce that the cell contains an N.

Next, look at the first cell in the second row. The box now has the letters E, N, R, and Z, so this cell can only contain M, A, K, I, or F. We can eliminate M and F by the row and K and M by the column, leaving only A and I. But both the second and third columns already have the letter I in them, so the I cannot be in either of those columns. Therefore, the cell must contain an I.

Turning to the second cell in the second row, we're down to M, A, K, or F as possibilities in the box. We can eliminate M and F by the row and nothing more by the column, leaving A and K. Using the same logic, we reach the same conclusion for the third cell in the second row. Now we know that those two cells contain the A and the K, but we don't know which is which. We'll have to come back to these cells later, as we solve more of the puzzle.

But in the meantime, this tells us that the second and third cells in the third row contain the last two letters in the box—M and F. But there is already an M in the second column. So those two cells contain the letters F and M, respectively. And we now have one letter of our missing clue word—we know the second letter is an M.

By repeating logic like this, we can eventually solve the entire puzzle. See page 7 for the answer.

Looking at the letters in the circled cells, we can fill in the clue to read "His novel AMERIKA was the first he wrote and the last one published." Looking at the letters in the shaded squares, we can find the final answer of writer FRANZ KAFKA.

There are 100 Who-doku puzzles in this book, ranging in difficulty from fairly easy at the beginning to pretty difficult at the end of the book. By the time you reach the end of the book, you'll have plenty of practice, but don't forget that knowing the clue and/or final answer can help you solve the puzzle. At the back of the book, you'll find two sets of hints. On pages 127 and 128, you can find the nationalities and occupations of the "Who" answers. (Nationalities of some celebrities change over time, so we've given the one most closely associated with the person.) On page 126, you'll find the clue words (the circled squares). This means that if you're really stuck and not having fun, you can get some help by looking up all or part of the clue words, which will fill in some more of the puzzle and hopefully help you get going again.

—Roy Leban

E	N	R	K	I	Z	A	F	M
I	A	K	M	F	R	E	Z	N
Z	F	M	N	E	A	R	I	K
K	I	F	E	Z	M	N	R	A
M	E	A	F	R	N	Z	K	I
N	R	Z	A	K	I	F	M	E
A	Z	N	I	M	F	K	E	R
R	K	I	Z	N	E	M	A	F
F	M	E	R	A	K	I	N	Z

1 He represented

GRAND RAPIDS

in the U.S. House.

```
S P R I N G F A D
```

P	S	D	A	I	F	N	G	R
F	N	I	P	R	G	D	S	A
G	R	A	N	D	S	P	F	X
A	F	R	S	N	I	G	P	D
D	I	G	F	P	R	S	A	N
S	P	N	D	G	A	R	I	F
N	G	R	R	A	P	I	D	S
I	D	S	G	F	N	A	R	P
R	A	P	X	S	D	F	N	G

GERALD

FORD

2 He was originally cast as the
TIN MAN.

| M | I | N | T | E | D | B | A | Y |

BUDDI
EBSEN

3 He lived in the

~~LAS VEGAS~~

Hilton for eight years.

| S | P | R | Y | G | A | V | E | L |

_ _ _ I _

_ _ _ _ _ _ _

4 Her father is

_ _ _ _ _ _ _ _ _ _ _ .

| A | N | K | H | V | I | S | O | R |

_ _ _ _ _

J _ _ E _

5 He led the

_ _ _ _ _ _   _ _ _ _ _ _ _

from 1961 to 1971.

N O T A D I E U S

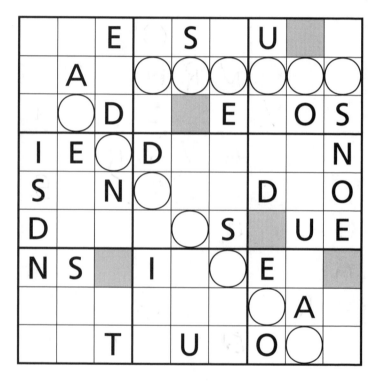

_   _ H _ _ _

6 He was in

_ _ _ _ _ _

for 27 years before being elected president.

S	L	I	M	A	P	R	O	N

_ E _ _ _ _

_ _ _ D E _ _

7 He is known as the cofounder of

_ _ _ _ _ _

(along with Georges Braque).

| M | O | S | A | I | C | P | U | B |

	P		A		I			
		A			O			
U	S		M					I
	B					U	C	S
	◯	◯	◯	◯	◯	◯		
S	M	O					B	
C					U		O	P
			S			B		
			C		B		M	

_ _ _ L _

_ _ _ _ _ _ _ _

8 He was a lifelong friend of fellow author HARPER LEE.

`M A R C H P E L T`

TRUMAN
CAPOTE

9 She was the first

— — — — —

actress to win the Academy Award for Best Actress.

E	L	K	C	R	Y	B	A	H

B					Y	A		R
		K						
R	H					K	L	E
	C				B		A	H
		R				L		
A	B		R				Y	
Y	R	C					E	A
					E			
K		H	A					L

— — — — —

— — — — — —

16

_ _ _ _ _ _ _ _ _ _ .

S	O	L	A	R	W	I	N	D

					L	S	I	
L	N						O	A
A		I			R			N
I			O	N			A	
							S	
	L			I	D.			W
R	I					N		O
N	W						R	
	A	L	S					

_ _ _ _ _ _ _

_ _ _ _ _ _

1 1 Some of his works were
inspired by British mathematician

_ _ _ _   _ _ _ _ _ _ _ .

| S | O | N | G | P | E | R | C | H |

M __

_ _ _ _ _ _

1 2 He was honored on a 2003 U.S. _STAMP_.

Z E S T C H A M P

C E S A R
C H A V E Z

He served as ambassador to

_ _ _ _ _ _

for nearly a decade.

C	R	A	B	K	N	I	F	E

	I	E						
C	◯		E			A		B
	N	◯	R			F		
			◯				C	R
			I	◯	F			
K	C				◯			
		I			R		E	
E		B			I			A
						N	F	

_ _ _ J _ M _ _

_ _ _ _ _ L _ _

20

1 4 He started his career doing caricatures in

_ _ _ _ _ _ _ _ .

| M | O | D | E | L | A | R | C | H |

_ _ _ U _ _
_ _ N _ T

1 5 He created two

_ _ _ _ _ _ _ _ _ _ _

for the Metropolitan Opera House in New York City.

O	R	A	L	M	U	S	I	C

A	S			R			U	
U	R	O		L				S
			O	S				I
R		L	◯	◯	◯	◯	◯	◯
			◯	C				
			◯			M		U
O			◯	I	C			
S			◯	M		U	C	A
	M		◯	U			L	O

_ _ _ _

_ H _ G _ _ _

22

1 6 She was one of 24 people to sign

_ _ _ _ _ _ 's

Declaration of Independence.

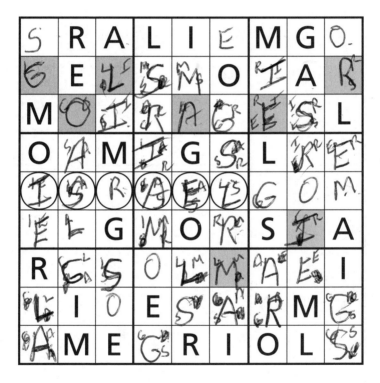

| G | L | A | M | O | R | I | S | E |

_ _ _ D _

_ _ _ _

His music was featured in
"The _ _ _ _ _ ."

| J | O | G | S | P | L | I | N | T |

		G		L				
L	J		N			P		G
		P			I		J	
							N	O
P		◯	◯	◯	◯	◯		J
G	N							
	T		I			J		
I		O			J		T	L
				S		N		

_ C _ _ _

_ _ _ _ _ _

1 **8** She is married to

_ _ _ _ _   _ _ _ _ _ _ .

| F | A | D | S | I | N | G | E | R |

	S	G	A	N	B	F	E	D
A						I	G	S
I				D		A		N
D			I				S	
F	E						N	I
	I				R			G
E				G		R	R	A
G	R	I		A	R			
N	A	S		R	E	G	I	

_ T _ _ _ _

_ _ _ _

"_ _ _ _   _ _ _ _ _ ."

| R | A | Y | B | L | E | N | D | S |

N				S			A	
◯	◯	◯	◯		Y	S	L	
Y				B				
E					R	Y	B	
		Y		◯		R		
	S	D	E		◯			L
				E		◯		N
	B	E	D				◯	
	Y			L				D

_ _ _

_ _ _ _ _ _

2 0 She painted some of her
most important works in

_ _ _ _ _ _ .

| C | A | M | P | S | T | Y | L | E |

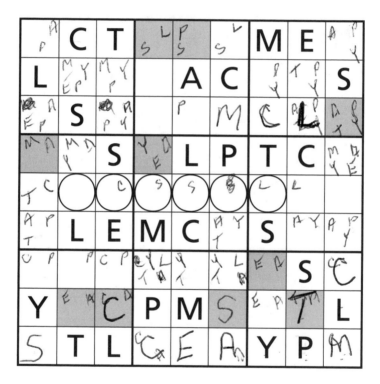

_ _ R _

_ _ _ _ _ _ _

2 1 His original name was

_ _ _ _ _ _ _   _ _ _ _ _ .

| C | H | I | A | S | Y | L | U | M |

Y	◯	I	H		L			
H	◯					M		
	U	◯	I				Y	
	A		U	◯	Y			
U				◯		C		
	S			H	◯	A		
L			C		I	◯		
I	◯	◯	◯	◯			U	
		I		S	C	L		

_ _ _ _ _ _ _ D

_ _ _

2 2 His

_ _ _ _ _   _ _ _ _ _

pokes fun at corporate America.

| R | I | P | M | A | S | C | O | T |

(grid)

						O	R	I
P	◯		O					
	I	◯		M			C	A
S	R	I	◯		◯			
	P			◯			M	
			◯		◯	I	P	T
O	A	◯		C			S	
	◯				R			M
I	M	R						

_ _ _ _ _

_ D _ _ _

He helped negotiate the

_ _ _ _ _ _ _ _ _ _ _

in 1993.

| C | O | L | D | T | R | A | Y | S |

A		T	D					
C	O					T	L	L
R		O		C	T	O		
			O	T	O	O		
Y		R	S	A	A	L		C
		L	Y	Y				
	O	Y	D					A
S	O	O						D
					O	C		R

_ _ _ I _
_ _ _ F _ _

2 4 His first professional team was the

_ _ _ _ _ _ _ _ Sharks.

| H | A | N | O | I | G | Y | M | S |

	G			I	H	O		
	○	M	Y		N	I	H	
		○	O	G				
	H	I	○				Y	
S				○				M
	M				○	A	I	
			S	Y	○			
	I	G	N		M	Y	○	
		S	G	H			N	○

_ _ _ _   _ _ _ _ _

2 5 She won a 1940 Academy Award without

_ _ _ _ _ _ _ .

| C | A | R | D | E | S | I | G | N |

_ _ _ _ _ _

_ O _ _ _ _

— — — — —   — — — — —

Walk of Fame.

| A | L | I | E | N | S | O | U | T |

L	U			O	I			
			S					I
○	○	○	○	○		E	▩	L
	T			S	N	L	U	
O					▩			E
I	S	N	U	▩	▩		T	
A		E	○	○	○	○	○	
U		▩	A				▩	
▩			S	U			E	O

— —   — —   — — — — —

2 7 Some of his most famous works are from

_ _ _ _ _ _ _ _ .

| S | T | E | A | M | Y | O | I | L |

		E	Y	S		M	L	
	○			L				
S		○	T	M				Y
	I	L	○					O
	T			○			S	
E					○	T	Y	
O				Y	E	○		L
			A				○	
	M	A		I	T	S		○

_ N _ _ _

_ D _ _ _

2 8 His

" _ _ _ _ _ _ _ _ "

of 1632 led to his conviction on charges of heresy.

| R | A | D | I | O | G | L | U | E |

○				A			R	
○			E	R	O		G	
○		E				U	L	
○	U	R	I					
○		D				I		
○					E	R	D	
○	D	I				O		
○	O		D	G	U			
	A			E				

_ _ _ _ _ _ _ _

_ _ _ _ _ _ _ _

_ _ _ _ _ .

| B | O | N | Y | H | I | K | E | R |

	O	B	H	▓				
H		Y	▓	▓	▓	R	O	
N		R		Y		▓		
			K		Y	▓		B
	E	○	○	○	○	○	H	
Y	▓		B		E			
				E		I	▓	R
	R	N	▓			B		Y
		▓			R	H	K	

_ _ _ _ _ _

_ _ S _ _

3 0 He was the first person to go into

— — — — — .

| G | U | I | T | A | R | B | O | Y |

R						O	A	
U				Y	T			
I	Y		R	○		U		
	I	O		○				
			T	○	G			
				○		Y	U	
		B	○	R			G	U
			U	A				R
	R	U						T

— — — —

— — — — — — N

3 1 He was the first

— — — — — — —

to win the Tour de France.

M I N G L E C A R

					A		M	
I	◯	R			E	N		C
C	N	◯			R			
			◯				C	I
		C	M	◯	N	E		
R	E				◯			
			R			◯	I	L
N		G	I			M	◯	E
	C		A					◯

— — — —

— — — O — D

3 2 He won a Golden Globe for his role in 1990's

"_ _ _ _ _   _ _ _ _."

| G | A | R | D | E | N | C | U | P |

○	D	U	R	A			C	
	○		C					
A	C	○		P				
	P	N	○					A
U		G		○		C		E
R		○				D	P	
		○		D			N	G
		○			N			
	N	○		C	U	P	A	

_ _ _ _ _
_ _ _ _ _ _ I _ _

39

_ _ _ _ _ _   _ _ _ _ .

| H | I | P | J | O | U | L | E | S |

			P		J	I		O
		S		H		E		
	○	○	○	○	○	○	J	U
	J	E			U		H	
			S					
	L		E		○	U	O	
L	S					○		
		U		L		J	○	
I		J	S		H			○

_ _ _ N

_ A _ _   _ _

" _ _ _ _ _ _ "

novels have been translated into more than 40 languages.

C	L	E	A	R	W	I	N	S

A		▓	L	I			W	
			C	N			R	
		◯				S		L
S	N	L	◯		▓	R	▓	
	W			◯			E	
▓		E			◯	L	S	A
W		R		▓		◯		▓
	E			S	I	▓	◯	
	S			A	W			E

— _ _ _ _ _ _ _ _ _ _ _

3 5 She is married to singer and songwriter

_ _ _ _ .

| E | L | M | H | A | I | K | U | S |

E				M				
K		S				M	E	
				H			A	K
L		M		K	S			
	H	◯	◯	◯	◯		K	
			I	U		H		L
S	A		M					
	K	E			A			U
				S				I

_ _ _ D _

_ _ _ _

— — — — — —

figure skater to win a World Championship.

M O D T R A I N S

— — — — — —

— — —

3 7 She codiscovered

_ _ _ _ _ _ .

| M | A | N | I | C | U | R | E | D |

	I	M	C				N	A
		U				C
U					E	R
D		◯				
	C		E	◯	N		M
			◯			R
	N	U			◯		C
	E			I	◯
I	D			C	A	E	◯

_ _ _ _ _

_ _ _ _ _

S H O W R E L I C

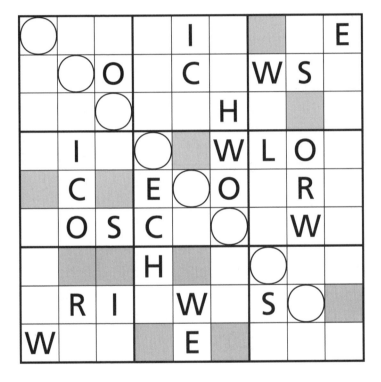

_ _ _ _ _
_ A _ _ _ _ _

3 9 He served as

_ _ _ _ _ _ _ _

prime minister for 15 years with a one-year gap.

R U I N E D C A P

					C	A		
I	◯						D	
D		◯			I		P	C
		D	◯	P			C	A
	E		I	◯	U		N	
N	A			C	◯	E		
A	N		C			◯		R
	P						◯	D
		I	A					◯

T _ _ _ _ _ _

40 He is affectionally referred to as

" _ _ _ _ _ _ _ _ _ ,"

reflecting his position in World War II.

| D | R | E | N | C | H | G | A | L |

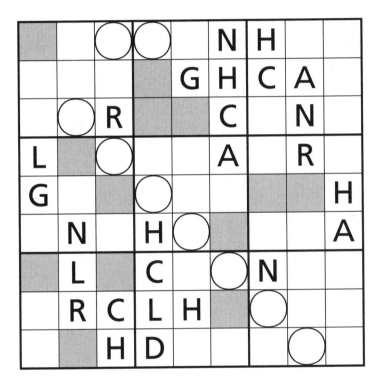

_ _ _ _ _ _ S

_ _ _ _ U _ _ _

4 1 He starred in the 1997 comedy
" _ _ _ _   _ _ _ _ ."

| J | A | I | L | M | E | R | C | Y |

C		E	M		Y			J
R		C			I			
	◯	◯	◯	◯		E		
	E			M				
L	M	A	C	I		Y	R	
	J				I			
Y		◯	◯	◯	◯			
	I			J		A		
R		E		C	J		I	

_ _ _

_ _ _ _ _ _

4 2 He took

_ _ _ _ _ _ _

State University to the NCAA basketball finals in 1979.

B	A	N	D	L	Y	R	I	C

C		B	Y	A	D	R		
R	◯							▓
		◯	I				C	
▓		Y	◯		▓		N	
A		D		◯		B	▓	L
	B		▓		◯	C		
	Y	▓			I	◯		
				▓		▓	◯	R
	▓	L	C	R	N	D		B

_ _ _ _ _

_ _ _ _

4 3 His portrait can be seen on the currency of

_ _ _ _ _ _ .

U	N	E	A	S	Y	W	I	T

A						E		I
				I		U	T	
N	◯			S	U		Y	W
I		◯	N				U	
		T	◯			Y		
	N			◯	S			T
T	I		W	Y	◯			U
	Y	S		U		◯		
W		U						Y

_ _ _

_ _ _ - _ _ _

4 4 He was featured on an episode of "The

_ _ _ _ _ _ _ _ ."

N	O	P	A	S	T	I	M	E

○	E				O		N
	○	S					A
O		○		E		T	
N		I	○A	M	S		
	O			○		N	
		A	N	E	○	T	P
	M		I			○	O
A					N	○	
I		O				M	

_ _ _ _

_ _ _ _ R _ _

____

to victory in their only Super Bowl appearance.

H	O	N	E	S	T	J	A	M

			M				A
					T	N	
O	T	(○) A			E	S	
S	N	(○)			O	H	
		H	(○) N				
H	M		(○)	J		N	
N	S			E	J	O	
	T	J					
M				O			

___ __ __

___ __ ___ __ __ __ __

4 6 His novel

" _ _ _   _ _ _ _ _   _ _ _ "

was turned into a TV movie starring Anthony Hopkins.

| N | I | G | H | T | M | A | R | E |

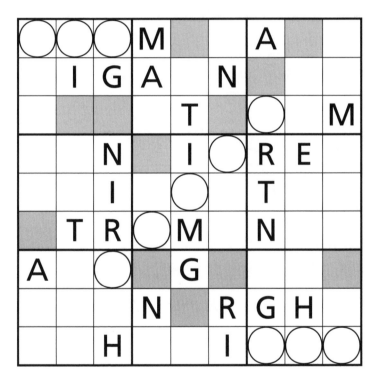

_ _ _ _ _

_ _ _ _ _ _

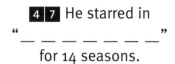

4 7 He starred in
" _ _ _ _ _ _ "
for 14 seasons.

| L | O | N | G | Z | E | B | R | A |

	A	R						
E		Z						
			E				O	B
N	B			O	R			E
	Z	A				R	B	
O			L	B			N	A
R	N				G			
						B		L
						O	R	

_ _ _ _ _   _ _ _ _ _ _

She is the only

_ _ _ _

actress to win the Academy Award for Best Actress.

F	I	L	M	E	D	A	R	T

D	T							
				I	F			
	L	F		◯				R
			T	◯	R	L	M	
		I		◯		R		
	E	R	M	◯	I			
A						F	L	
			D	M				
							E	A

_ _ _ _ _ _

_ _ _ _ _ N

4 9 He has not owned a

— — —

in over 50 years.

L A N D P E R C H

		H	A				L	
C	L					H		E
P		N						
A	N		◯		D			
D			H	◯	L			N
			E		◯		D	A
						N		H
L		P					C	D
	C				H	L		

— — — — — —

— — — — — —

5 0 He spent five years as a

_ _ _ _ _ _ _ _

in Nashville.

| P | E | T | R | O | L | G | A | S |

○	O	S	T					
	○G		A	P		O		
T		○L					R
	T	E	○			G	A
				○			
A	R			○	L	P	
S				R	○		O
	P		S	O		T	○	
				E	P	S	

_ _ _ _ _ _

He played the host of the fictional TV show

" _ _ _ _   _ _ _ _ . "

| E | M | U | L | A | T | I | O | N |

	A		N		U		
			I	E				M
				A			L	E
U	O							A
M			U	O	T			L
L							N	U
O	U		L					
A			M	O				
		L		U		I		

_ _ _   _ _ _ _ _

5 2 She started playing

_ _ _ _ _ _

at the age of six and won her
first tournament at the age of nine.

| S | M | E | L | T | C | O | I | N |

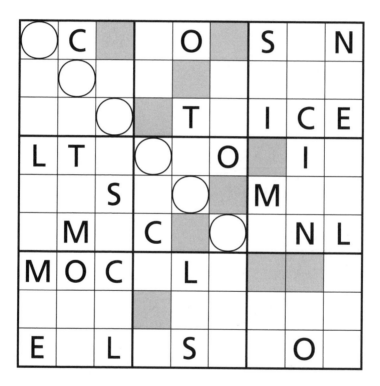

_ _ _ _ _ A

_ _ _ _ _

_ _ _ _ _ _ _ _-born

figure skater won Gold at the 1994 Olympics.

B	U	N	K	O	L	I	A	R

		L			U	A		
	O		O			K		L
		O					N	U
	N	O	O					A
	R	I	L	O	O	N	K	
A					O	R	O	
B	A					O		
I		N			K		O	
		R	U			O		O

_ _ S _ _ _

_ _ _ _ _

5 4 His fourth wife was

_ _ _ _   _ _ _ _ _ _ .

| G | A | N | T | R | Y | D | O | C |

O						C		N
◯	◯	◯	◯	C	O		R	
N	C	G		D				
		◯					A	
T		D	◯			G		O
	R			◯				
				G	◯	Y	C	A
	D		R	A		◯		
G		Y					◯	D

_ _ _ _

_ _ _ _ _

5 5 She is most famous for her

_ _ _ _ _ _ _ ,

which spanned 60 years.

V	I	N	E	Y	A	R	D	S

			S	N				D
R	(N)			E		Y		
	(D)			R		E		
E	(O)				R			
	Y	(V)						
	R		(O)			A		
I	V		D	(O)				
E	N			I	(Y)			
Y			E	S				

_ _ _ _ _ _   _ _ _

5 6 He is undoubtedly credited with far more

— — — — — —

than he actually wrote.

| F | L | O | P | B | E | A | D | S |

L		F		B				A
				A	E	O		
S	A	L	E			F		
			◯	◯	◯	◯	◯	◯
		E			O	P	A	D
	D	P	B					
O				D		S		L

— — — — — —

57 His nickname was

"_ _ _ - _ _ _ _."

CRINGEJOB

	C			E			I	O
G								
		J	C		R			
	G					I	B	C
N	◯	◯	◯	◯	◯	◯	◯	J
J	B	R					O	
			N		I	G		
								N
O	N		G			C		

_ _ _ _

_ _ _ _

5 **8** He was one of the first people to write about

_ _ _ _ _ _ .

| A | R | T | C | H | I | S | E | L |

	I		E	C		S		
			S	R	E	A		
	S	◯						
I	E		◯	A				
		T		◯		A		
				R	◯		E	S
						◯	H	
	T	C	I	E			◯	
		H			L	S		R

_ _ _ _ _ O _ _ _

5 **9** Her TV show theme song was

"_ _ _   _ _ _ _ _ ,   _ _ _ _ _ ."

S O D A Q U E R Y

				D		O	Q	S
O	S			Y	R			E
◯	◯	◯						
A					D	Q		R
	Q	◯	◯	◯			U	
E		Y	O					D
					◯	◯	◯	◯
S			R	U			O	Q
R	D	O		E				

_ _ _   I _   _ _ _ _

6 0 He was married to

_ _ _ _ _ _ _ _ _ _ _ _ .

L A R G E W I N D

○	○	○	○	○		W	N	▨
			I					E
E		○		G			D	
D	R		○	W			▨	
	E	N		○		I	A	
			L	○			G	D
	L			R	○			N
N	▨	▨	▨	▨	D		○	
	A	W	▨	▨	▨	▨		

_ _ _ _

_ _ _ _ _ _

_ _ _ _ _ _ _ _ _ .

| I | N | M | Y | S | T | O | R | E |

			N					
			M		T	N	S	
T			E				M	I
R	I	S						
		N				R		
						M	I	Y
O	E				M			T
	Y	T	S		E			
					O			

_ A _ _ L _ _

_ _ _ _ _ _

6 2 "The Miraculous Mandarin" and
"The Wooden Prince" were two of his

__ __ __ __ __ __ __ .

| S | O | B | E | R | T | A | L | K |

				A			S	
		E		S		T		O
								K
	S	O		B	R		K	
K	R		O		S		L	T
	E		A	K		O	R	
O								
E		T		O		R		
	L			R				

__ __ __ __

__ __ __ __ __ __

6 3 Her real first name is

_ _ _ _ .

| G | I | Z | M | O | B | A | R | S |

				A	B			
B	Z		G	I				
		M					B	
	B	Z		M	G	I		A
	◯	◯	◯	◯				
A		I	Z	B		G	R	
	R					M		
				O	R		A	G
			I	S				

_ _   _ _ _ _ _

6 4 She is married to American gymnast

_ _ _ _   _ _ _ _ _ _ _ .

| B | A | R | N | O | T | I | C | E |

				B		R		A
I		◯	◯	◯	◯		O	
O			I			T	B	E
◯	R						T	O
T	◯		R		E			C
E	B	◯				A		
R	T	E	◯		I			B
	I		◯					T
B		C		O	◯			

_ _ D _ _

_ _ M _ _ _ _ _

6 5 His first book was the autobiographical
"_ _ _ _ _."

| N | E | W | L | I | G | H | T | S |

	W		L					
L	E						T	N
		◯	G	H				
			◯		N			T
	H	T		◯		E	I	
S			T		◯			
				W	G	◯		
W	N						H	I
					S		L	

_ _ _ _

_ _ _ _ _ _

He speaks several languages
in addition to his native

_ _ _ _ _ _ .

| R | O | M | A | N | B | I | K | E |

R	M		B			A		
E			K	N				O
		I		R			E	
	E		O					
I	◯	◯	◯	◯	◯	◯		B
					N		K	
	I			A		E		
N				I	R			A
		B			O		N	I

_ _ _

_ _ - _ _ _ _

His 1938 radio broadcast of a novel by

_. _. _ _ _ _ _

gained him international notoriety.

H E N S G R O W L

			R			H		
						S	W	N
◯		◯	N	E	W			L
N	O			◯				G
	L	H			◯	W	N	
W						◯	O	H
E			G	H	N		◯	
L	H	N						◯
		O			S			

_ _ _ _ _ _ _ _ _ _

_ _ _ _ _ _ _ _ _ _ _ _

He was known as a master of

_ _ _ _ _ _ _ _ .

GUIDANCES

		N		G				U
		A	E	C			D	
U						G	I	
I	S							
			D		A			
							N	E
	A	C						N
	D			A	C	U		
S				E		A		

_ L _ _

_ _ _ _ _ _ _ _

____ _____

record label in 1974.

A	S	K	H	E	R	D	O	G

		H	O			K	G	
R	K		G		D	A		
		◯	◯	◯	◯			H
D		H						S
	H		S			R		
O				E				D
A			◯	◯	◯	◯	◯	
	E	K	A				O	G
	R	O			G	A		

____ ____

____ I __ __ N

He received an honorary

— — — — —

in 2003.

| A | L | E | R | T | C | O | P | S |

			L			C		
	◯				P	L	R	S
		◯	O				P	
T		R	◯	E		P	A	O
		P		◯		R		
O	A	L		P	◯	E		T
	T				S			
A	L	E	R					
		C			A			

— — — — —

_ _ ' _ _ _ _ _

— — — — — — — .

| M | A | P | V | E | N | D | O | R |

	D					O		
◯				V				
N	◯	V		R		M		P
O		◯	M		A		N	V
	N		◯				M	
V	E		R	◯	D			A
P		E		A	◯	V		O
		V			◯			
		O					E	

— — — —   — — — — —

7 2 He taught at the

_ _ _ _ _ _ _

school of art and architecture.

| B | U | L | K | H | E | A | P | S |

L				K	P	S		A
	K			U	L		P	
				S				
E							H	
	K	S				P	A	
	U							L
			B					
	L		P	A		E		
U		P	S	E				B

_ _ _ _   _ _ _ _

He chased Arnold Schwarzenegger in the movie

" _ _ _ _ _ _ ."

| N | I | C | E | R | J | A | M | S |

N		C		R			S	
R			C					
		(O)			N		J	
A			(O)	I			C	
E	J		N	(O)	C		I	R
	R			J	(O)			A
	C		S			(O)		
					I		(O)	N
	E			N		C		I

_ _ _ _ _ _

_ _ _ _

7 4 He is best known today for his

_ _ _ _ _ _ _ .

O V A L T I R E S

		R				S	
T	O					A	
E	L		S				V
		S	E	L	O	I	
R							L
	E	L	A	O		T	
L				A		T	I
	R						O
		E				V	

_ _ _ _ _ _ _ _

__ __ __ __ __ __ __

novels feature a Polish-Italian-American protagonist.

| S | P | Y | M | A | R | K | E | T |

E				M		Y		P
	◯							S
	K	◯			S		T	
	E		◯		K	T	R	
		M	Y	◯	R	P		
	R	K	M		◯		S	
	S		E			◯	P	
M							◯	
R		E		S				T

__ __ __ __

__ __ __ __ __ __ __ __

_ _ _ _   _ _ _ _ _ .

| B | I | G | O | R | A | C | L | E |

			L	I	O			E
	C			A		B		
◯	◯	◯	◯			L		
R	B	A	E	O		I		
		E		L	C	O	R	A
		C		◯	◯	◯	◯	◯
		R			E		O	
A				I	C	R		

_ _ _ _ _ _

_ _ W _ _ _

7 7 He has an

_ _ _ _ _ _ _

named after him.

| T | R | O | J | A | N | P | I | E |

E			T			A	P	
	◯			O	P			R
		◯		J				
		P	◯				E	
I		A		◯		T		O
	T				◯	J		
				T		◯		
A			O	I		◯		
	P	R			E			J

_ _ H _

L _ _ _ _ _

7 8 His life was the basis for a novel by

— — — — — — — .

G	A	L	U	M	P	H	I	N

H	U				M		A
	U			I			
	L		M	U	H		I
	G	H					
		I		N			
				N	L		
U	M	N	I		P		
		H					
I	P					H	U

— — — —

— — — — — — —

C O Z Y M E D A L

	L			A				Y
◯					O	D		C
Z	◯				Y	M		
C		◯	Y					
	M	E	◯			L	Z	
			◯	A				D
	D	E		◯				Z
E		L	A		◯			
M				Y			D	

_ _ I _ _

_ _ _ _

He won his first Oscar for the 1977 film

" _ _ _ _ _   _ _ _ _ . "

A	W	H	I	L	E	Y	O	N

				◯	H	Y		W
	E		◯		Y			
		◯		O		I	E	H
O	◯				W			A
◯		Y	◯	N		W		
E			O	◯				L
I	A	E		H	◯			
			E			◯	A	
N		L	A					

_ _ _ D _

_ _ _ _ _

8 1 He famously claimed that he was not a

_ _ _ _ _ _ _ .

S H O R T C A K E

	K							
	(O)	S		O		K		
R	O	( )		K	S			H
			( )		O		K	
T		H	K	( )	E	O		R
	E		S		( )			
K			O	H		( )	C	T
		T		A		S	( )	
							H	

_ _ _ _ _ _ _ _

82 He was the

_ _ _ _ _ _ _ _ _

of the Rock and Roll Hall of Fame.

C H E A P T R I M

			C			T	P	
H	O			M	A	C		
	M	O	I					
T		R	O	C	M			
			O					
			E	A	O	H		P
					C	O	M	
		P	T	E			O	A
	E	A			R			O

_ _ _ _ _

8 3 He named his son

— — — — —

after his close friend and collaborator.

| S | T | E | A | M | I | R | O | N |

T	O		M	E				S
	S				A	N		
		◯		O		M		
			◯	S			I	
N				◯				A
	M		T		◯			
		N		R		◯		
		M	I				E	
I				A	T		M	O

— — — —

— — — — — — — —

8 4 Scarlett Johansson played his

_ _ _ _ _ _ _

in the 2003 movie "Girl With a Pearl Earring."

| R | V | S | E | N | T | J | A | M |

V	N				R		A	
		A	V					
		M		S			N	
N		T		M	J			
	○	○	○	○	○	○	○	
			T	S		A		J
E			A			V		
					E	T		
	T		N				R	E

_ _ _ _

_ _ _ _ _ _ _ _

8 5 He created more than 1,500 paintings
in his career, most of them

— — — — — — — .

| V | A | L | I | D | R | U | S | E |

R	◯	I	L		U	D	E	V
V		◯						A
			◯		V	I		
D				◯		E		
	I	A			◯	R	U	
		R				◯		L
		E	D				◯	
I								E
L	U	D	E		R	V		I

— — — — — — O —

— — — —

When he coined the word

— — — — — — — — ,

he thought it was already a word.

B	O	R	I	C	V	A	T	S

			T		A	C		O
T	V				S		I	
	C							V
	V					S	O	
		S		C				
	O	B					A	
B						V		
	I		R			B		A
V		R	C		I			

— — — — —

— — — M — —

— — — — — —

on "Friends."

L	O	U	D	T	I	G	E	R

	◯	R		E				
	◯	D				G		R
I	U		◯	R	G	O	E	
G		T	◯			O		
	I				◯		G	
	E			D	◯			L
	D	G	O	T			U	E
U		I			R			
			D		L			

— — — — — —

— — — — — —

88 His artwork is known for drawing from fantasy,

— — — — — — ,

and the irrational.

| M | A | Y | R | E | J | O | I | N |

A	I	J	Y	R		O		
	E							A
		R	J			M	○	
			I			○	O	
			N	○				
	Y		○	E				
		I	○		J	Y		
E		○					I	
		N		A	I	E	J	R

— — — — — — — — —

8 9 He led the University of

_ _ _ _ _ _

to the NCAA basketball championship in 1988.

M	Y	K	I	D	S	A	N	G

I			K	M				
			S			D		
A		◯	D			I	M	G
			◯				I	M
	M	D		◯		Y	A	
G	I				◯			
S	K	Y			I	◯		N
		I			K		◯	
			G		Y			I

_ _ _ _ _ _

_ _ _ _ _ _ _

His chosen last name means "thunder" in

_ _ _ _ _ _ .

| B | U | D | H | A | W | K | E | R |

U		D	W					
		R		H				
		◯		E	U			D
R		W◯			K			H
D		K		◯		U		E
B			H		◯	D		W
W			U	K		◯		
				A		B	◯	
					B	H		K

_ _ _ _

_ _ _ _ _

Her eponymous scoring method is used to determine the health of

__ __ __ __ __ __ .

B	I	G	R	A	V	E	N	S

S			E	G				
◯		I	S		R	E		
	◯	E		N				
E		◯					N	G
N		A	◯	B		R		E
G	R			◯				V
				A	◯	V		
		N	V		B	S		
				R	E			B

__ __ __ __ __ __ __ __

__ P __ __ __

She starred as a skiing instructor in the 1937 film
" _ _ _ _   _ _ _ ."

| C | H | I | N | A | J | E | T | S |

C	N		H					
	I	A	S					
E	O	O	O	O		C		
		J	N				E	
		I	T		J	S		
	A				H	J		
		T		O	O	O		S
					S	A	N	
					N		T	C

_ O _ _ _

_ _ _ _ _

His specialty was the "art of
_ _ _ _ _ _ _ ."

| C | A | L | M | S | I | R | E | N |

_ _ _ _ _ _

_ _ _ _ _ _ U

Many people mistakenly think that his first name is

_ _ _ _ _ _ _ .

D	O	I	N	G	M	A	T	H

N		I			T		H	
				I	A	T		D
	H			G		N		
	M	O		I	G			
	G		N			D		
O		D	I	M				
	I		G			H		M

_ _ _ _ _ _ _ S

_ _ _ _ _ _

He is perhaps the world's best-known

_ _ _ _ _   _ _ _ _ _ _ _ .

| C | A | M | P | Y | L | O | R | E |

_ _ · _ _   _ _

9 **6** He hit 14 home runs for the

— — — — — — —

in 2005.

| M | A | Y | O | R | L | I | E | S |

◯	E		I	R	Y	A	
	◯ L			▓	▓		
	▓	◯		O		R	S
		◯	M				Y
R		S	◯	A			E
A	▓	I	▓	◯		▓	
E	Y	R			◯		
▓		▓			E	▓	
	M	A	E	S	I		

— — — — —

— — — —

103

9 7 He was the first

_ _ _ _   _ _ _ _ _ _

to visit Israel.

| E | N | D | S | B | R | A | W | L |

		D			S	E		A
	S			D	(W)	W		L
(O)	N		W	(O)		B		
S	(O)	(O)						
		(O)	L	R	E			
	(O)		(O)					N
(O)	D			B		E		
R		S		L		D		
E		W	S			B		

_ _ _ _ _

_ _ _ _ T

His childhood dreams of

_ _ _ _ _ _ _ _

inspired his well-known children's book.

| C | O | L | D | E | R | H | A | T |

	D		O	L				
L		R			E		C	
A								D
	T	D						
	C		H		T		A	
						C	E	
T								L
	L		R			H		C
				T	C		R	

_ _ _ _

_ _ _ _

_ _ _ _ _ _

can often be found in science centers.

A N T I L O C K S

I	O				K	C		
	S		I	C				
A	L				T		I	
			K			O	T	
			◯	◯	◯	◯	◯	
	N	L			S			
	A		T				N	I
				A	O		C	
		T	N				O	K

_ _ _ _ _ _ _

_ E _ _ _

His father wanted him to be a

_ _ _ _ _ _ ,
not a painter.

| G | R | A | Y | W | E | L | D | S |

			Y					
	◯	E		D			R	A
S		◯		W	E	Y		
L	A	S	◯					D
				◯				
R				◯	G	A	W	
	G	Y	S		◯			E
D	R			A		S		
					R			

_ _ _ _ _

_ _ _ _ _ _

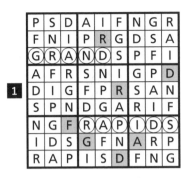

1

P	S	D	A	I	F	N	G	R
F	N	I	P	R	G	D	S	A
G	R	A	N	D	S	P	F	I
A	F	R	S	N	I	G	P	D
D	I	G	F	P	R	S	A	N
S	P	N	D	G	A	R	I	F
N	G	F	R	A	P	I	D	S
I	D	S	G	F	N	A	R	P
R	A	P	I	S	D	F	N	G

Gerald Ford

2

D	I	A	M	B	E	T	N	Y
T	E	B	Y	D	N	M	I	A
M	N	Y	T	A	I	B	E	D
E	B	T	I	N	D	A	Y	M
N	A	M	E	Y	T	D	B	I
I	Y	D	B	M	A	N	T	E
A	T	N	D	E	Y	I	M	B
Y	M	I	A	T	B	E	D	N
B	D	E	N	I	M	Y	A	T

Buddy Ebsen

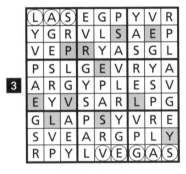

3

L	A	S	E	G	P	Y	V	R
Y	G	R	V	L	S	A	E	P
V	E	P	R	Y	A	S	G	L
P	S	L	G	E	V	R	Y	A
A	R	G	Y	P	L	E	S	V
E	Y	V	S	A	R	L	P	G
G	L	A	P	S	Y	V	R	E
S	V	E	A	R	G	P	L	Y
R	P	Y	L	V	E	G	A	S

Elvis Presley

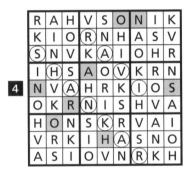

4

R	A	H	V	S	O	N	I	K
K	I	O	R	N	H	A	S	V
S	N	V	K	A	I	O	H	R
I	H	S	A	O	V	K	R	N
N	V	A	H	R	K	I	O	S
O	K	R	N	I	S	H	V	A
H	O	N	S	K	R	V	A	I
V	R	K	I	H	A	S	N	O
A	S	I	O	V	N	R	K	H

Norah Jones

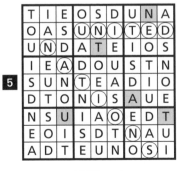

5

T	I	E	O	S	D	U	N	A
O	A	S	U	N	I	T	E	D
U	N	D	A	T	E	I	O	S
I	E	A	D	O	U	S	T	N
S	U	N	T	E	A	D	I	O
D	T	O	N	I	S	A	U	E
N	S	U	I	A	O	E	D	T
E	O	I	S	D	T	N	A	U
A	D	T	E	U	N	O	S	I

U Thant

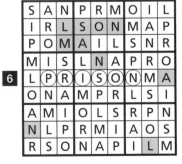

6

S	A	N	P	R	M	O	I	L
I	R	L	S	O	N	M	A	P
P	O	M	A	I	L	S	N	R
M	I	S	L	N	A	P	R	O
L	P	R	I	S	O	N	M	A
O	N	A	M	P	R	L	S	I
A	M	I	O	L	S	R	P	N
N	L	P	R	M	I	A	O	S
R	S	O	N	A	P	I	L	M

Nelson Mandela

7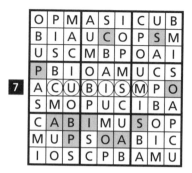

Pablo Picasso

8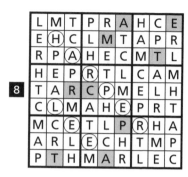

Truman Capote

9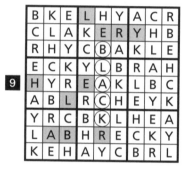

Halle Berry

10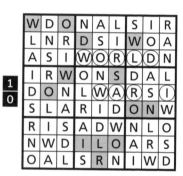

Woodrow Wilson

11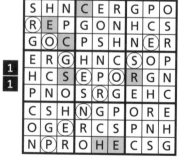

M.C. Escher

12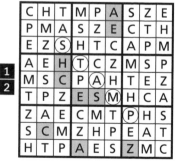

Cesar Chavez

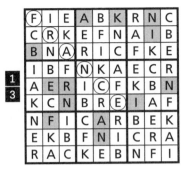

13

Benjamin Franklin

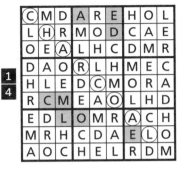

14

Claude Monet

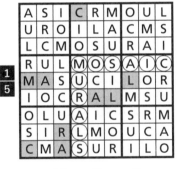

15

Marc Chagall

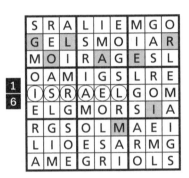

16

Golda Meir

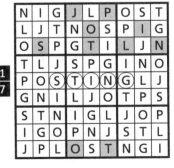

17

Scott Joplin

18

Steffi Graf

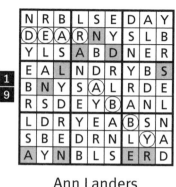

Ann Landers

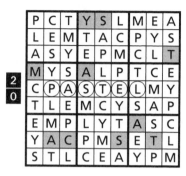

Mary Cassatt

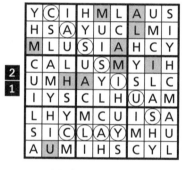

Muhammad Ali

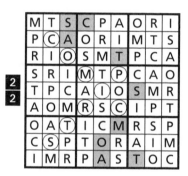

Scott Adams

Yasir Arafat

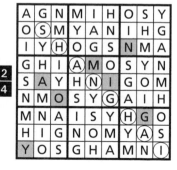

Yao Ming

25

D	N	S	G	A	C	E	I	R
A	R	E	I	N	S	C	G	D
G	C	I	R	D	E	N	S	A
C	A	D	E	R	I	S	N	G
S	E	N	D	C	G	A	R	I
R	I	G	N	S	A	D	E	C
I	S	A	C	G	N	R	D	E
E	D	C	S	I	R	G	A	N
N	G	R	A	E	D	I	C	S

Ginger Rogers

26

L	U	T	E	O	I	S	A	N
N	E	O	L	S	A	T	U	I
S	A	I	N	T	U	E	O	L
E	T	A	O	I	S	N	L	U
O	L	U	A	N	T	I	S	E
I	S	N	U	E	L	O	T	A
A	N	E	T	L	O	U	I	S
U	O	S	I	A	E	L	N	T
T	I	L	S	U	N	A	E	O

T.S. Eliot

27

I	A	E	Y	S	O	M	L	T
T	Y	M	E	A	L	O	I	S
S	L	O	T	M	I	A	E	Y
A	I	L	S	T	Y	E	M	O
M	T	Y	O	E	A	L	S	I
E	O	S	I	L	M	T	Y	A
O	S	T	M	Y	E	I	A	L
L	E	I	A	O	S	Y	T	M
Y	M	A	L	I	T	S	O	E

Ansel Adams

28

D	G	O	U	A	L	E	R	I
I	L	U	E	R	O	D	G	A
A	R	E	G	I	D	U	L	O
L	U	R	I	D	A	G	O	E
O	E	D	R	U	G	I	A	L
G	I	A	L	O	E	R	D	U
U	D	I	A	L	R	O	E	G
E	O	L	D	G	U	A	I	R
R	A	G	O	E	I	L	U	D

Galileo Galilei

29

E	O	B	H	R	K	N	Y	I
H	K	Y	N	B	I	R	O	E
N	I	R	E	Y	O	K	B	H
R	N	O	K	H	Y	E	I	B
B	E	I	R	O	N	Y	H	K
Y	H	K	B	I	E	O	R	N
K	Y	H	O	E	B	I	N	R
O	R	N	I	K	H	B	E	Y
I	B	E	Y	N	R	H	K	O

Henrik Ibsen

30

R	B	T	G	U	I	O	A	Y
U	O	A	B	Y	T	G	R	I
I	Y	G	R	O	A	U	T	B
G	I	O	Y	R	U	T	B	A
A	U	Y	T	B	G	R	I	O
B	T	R	A	I	O	Y	U	G
Y	A	B	O	T	R	I	G	U
T	G	I	U	A	Y	B	O	R
O	R	U	I	G	B	A	Y	T

Yuri Gagarin

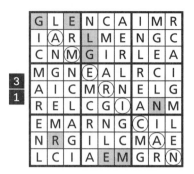

3 1

Greg LeMond

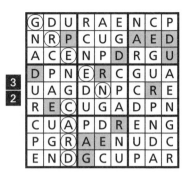

3 2

Gérard Depardieu

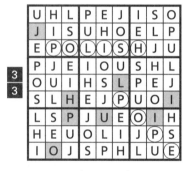

3 3

John Paul II

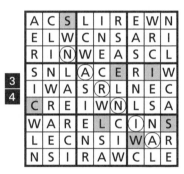

3 4

C.S. Lewis

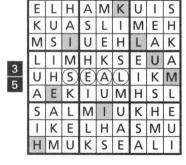

3 5

Heidi Klum

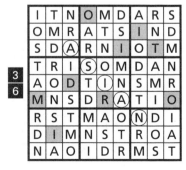

3 6

Midori Ito

37

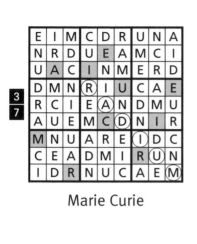

Marie Curie

38

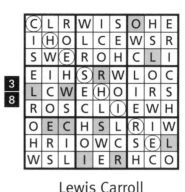

Lewis Carroll

39

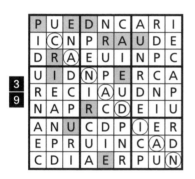

Pierre Trudeau

40

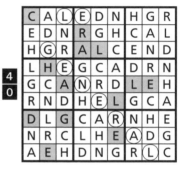

Charles de Gaulle

41

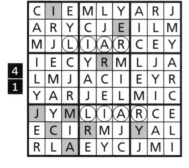

Jim Carrey

42

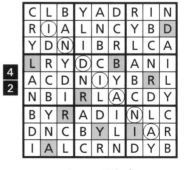

Larry Bird

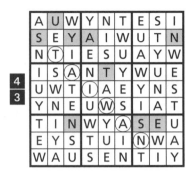

4 3

Sun Yat-sen

4 4

Pete Sampras

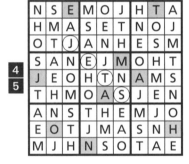

4 5

Joe Namath

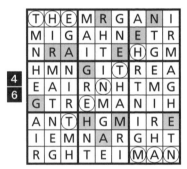

4 6

Graham Greene

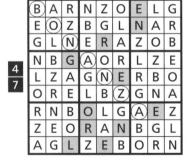

4 7

Lorne Greene

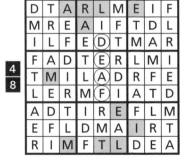

4 8

Marlee Matlin

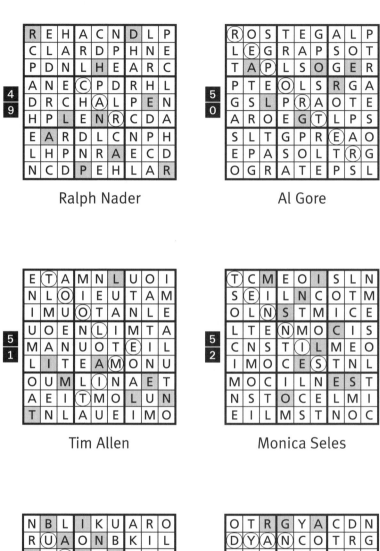

49 — Ralph Nader

```
R E H A C N D L P
C L A R D P H N E
P D N L H E A R C
A N E C P D R H L
D R C H A L P E N
H P L E N R C D A
E A R D L C N P H
L H P N R A E C D
N C D P E H L A R
```

Ralph Nader

50 — Al Gore

```
R O S T E G A L P
L E G R A P S O T
T A P L S O G E R
P T E O L S R G A
G S L P R A O T E
A R O E G T L P S
S L T G P R E A O
E P A S O L T R G
O G R A T E P S L
```

Al Gore

51 — Tim Allen

```
E T A M N L U O I
N L O I E U T A M
I M U O T A N L E
U O E N L I M T A
M A N U O T E I L
L I T E A M O N U
O U M L I N A E T
A E I T M O L U N
T N L A U E I M O
```

Tim Allen

52 — Monica Seles

```
T C M E O I S L N
S E I L N C O T M
O L N S T M I C E
L T E N M O C I S
C N S T I L M E O
I M O C E S T N L
M O C I L N E S T
N S T O C E L M I
E I L M S T N O C
```

Monica Seles

53 — Oksana Baiul

```
N B L I K U A R O
R U A O N B K I L
O I K A R L B N U
K N O R B I L U A
U R I L A O N K B
A L B K U N R O I
B A U N O R I L K
I O N B L K U A R
L K R U I A O B N
```

Oksana Baiul

54 — Cary Grant

```
O T R G Y A C D N
D Y A N C O T R G
N C G T D R A O Y
Y G C O T D N A R
T N D A R C G Y O
A R O Y N G D T C
R O T D G N Y C A
C D N R A Y O G T
G A Y C O T R N D
```

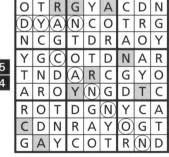

Cary Grant

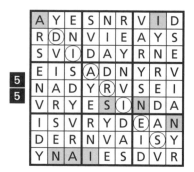

Anaïs Nin

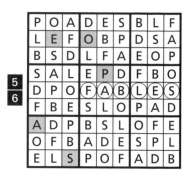

Aesop

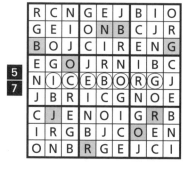

Björn Borg

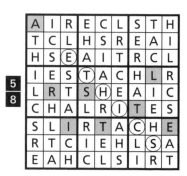

Aristotle

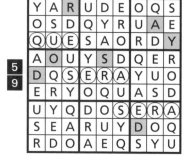

Doris Day

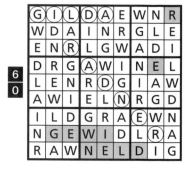

Gene Wilder

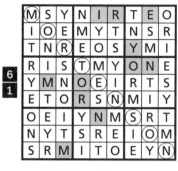

61 Marilyn Monroe

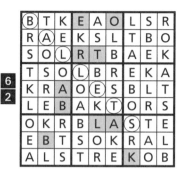

62 Béla Bartók

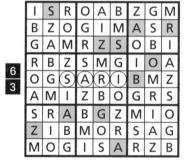

63 Zsa Zsa Gabor

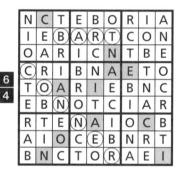

64 Nadia Comaneci

65 Elie Wiesel

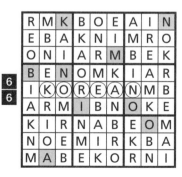

66 Ban Ki-Moon

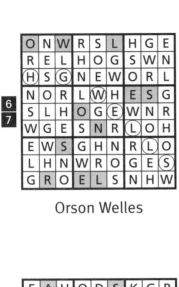

6/7

6/8

Orson Welles

Alec Guinness

6/9

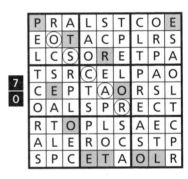

7/0

George Harrison

Peter O'Toole

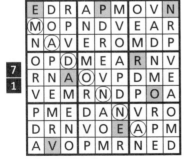

7/1

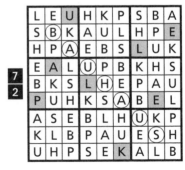

7/2

Eva Perón

Paul Klee

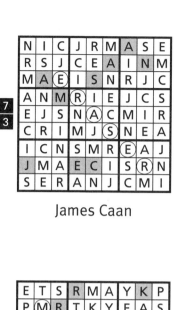

James Caan

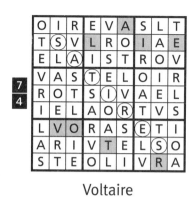

Voltaire

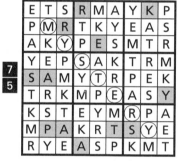

Sara Paretsky

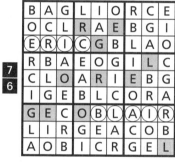

George Orwell

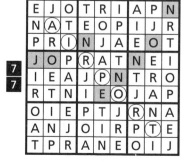

John Lennon

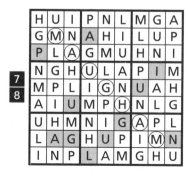

Paul Gauguin

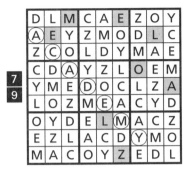

79

Émile Zola

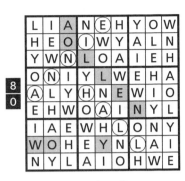

80

Woody Allen

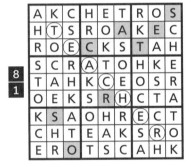

81

Socrates

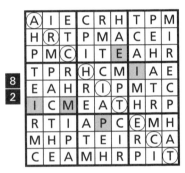

82

I.M. Pei

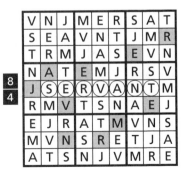

83

Eero Saarinen

84

Jan Vermeer

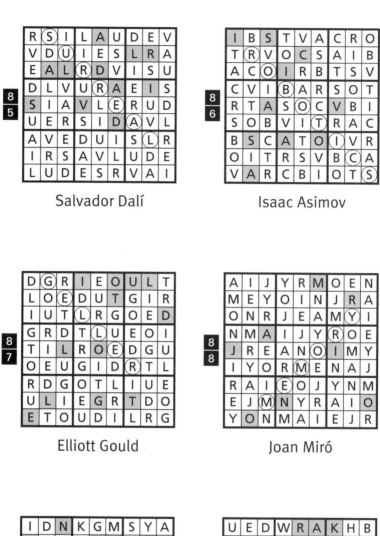

8 / 5

R	S	I	L	A	U	D	E	V
V	D	U	I	E	S	L	R	A
E	A	L	R	D	V	I	S	U
D	L	V	U	R	A	E	I	S
S	I	A	V	L	E	R	U	D
U	E	R	S	I	D	A	V	L
A	V	E	D	U	I	S	L	R
I	R	S	A	V	L	U	D	E
L	U	D	E	S	R	V	A	I

Salvador Dalí

8 / 6

I	B	S	T	V	A	C	R	O
T	R	V	O	C	S	A	I	B
A	C	O	I	R	B	T	S	V
C	V	I	B	A	R	S	O	T
R	T	A	S	O	C	V	B	I
S	O	B	V	I	T	R	A	C
B	S	C	A	T	O	I	V	R
O	I	T	R	S	V	B	C	A
V	A	R	C	B	I	O	T	S

Isaac Asimov

8 / 7

D	G	R	I	E	O	U	L	T
L	O	E	D	U	T	G	I	R
I	U	T	L	R	G	O	E	D
G	R	D	T	L	U	E	O	I
T	I	L	R	O	E	D	G	U
O	E	U	G	I	D	R	T	L
R	D	G	O	T	L	I	U	E
U	L	I	E	G	R	T	D	O
E	T	O	U	D	I	L	R	G

Elliott Gould

8 / 8

A	I	J	Y	R	M	O	E	N
M	E	Y	O	I	N	J	R	A
O	N	R	J	E	A	M	Y	I
N	M	A	I	J	Y	R	O	E
J	R	E	A	N	O	I	M	Y
I	Y	O	R	M	E	N	A	J
R	A	I	E	O	J	Y	N	M
E	J	M	N	Y	R	A	I	O
Y	O	N	M	A	I	E	J	R

Joan Miró

8 / 9

I	D	N	K	G	M	S	Y	A
M	Y	G	S	I	A	D	N	K
A	S	K	D	Y	N	I	M	G
Y	N	S	A	K	D	G	I	M
K	M	D	I	N	G	Y	A	S
G	I	A	Y	M	S	N	K	D
S	K	Y	M	D	I	A	G	N
D	G	I	N	A	K	M	S	Y
N	A	M	G	S	Y	K	D	I

Danny Manning

9 / 0

U	E	D	W	R	A	K	H	B
A	B	R	K	H	D	W	E	U
K	W	H	B	E	U	R	A	D
R	U	W	E	D	K	A	B	H
D	H	K	A	B	W	U	R	E
B	A	E	H	U	R	D	K	W
W	R	B	U	K	H	E	D	A
H	K	U	D	A	E	B	W	R
E	D	A	R	W	B	H	U	K

Ehud Barak

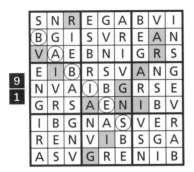

9/1

Virginia Apgar

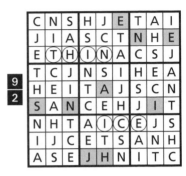

9/2

Sonja Henie

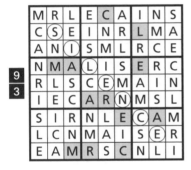

9/3

Marcel Marceau

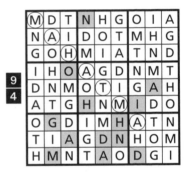

9/4

Mohandas Gandhi

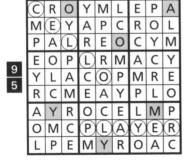

9/5

Yo-Yo Ma

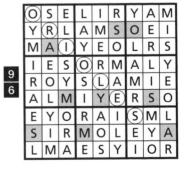

9/6

Sammy Sosa

124

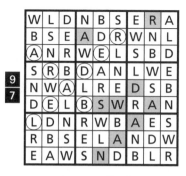

97

Anwar Sadat

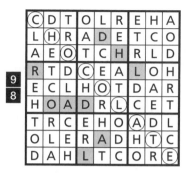

98

Roald Dahl

99

Nikola Tesla

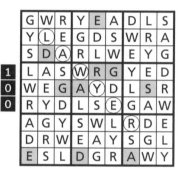

100

Edgar Degas

HINTS (circled squares)

1. GRAND RAPIDS
2. TIN MAN
3. LAS VEGAS
4. RAVI SHANKAR
5. UNITED NATIONS
6. PRISON
7. CUBISM
8. HARPER LEE
9. BLACK
10. WORLD WAR I
11. ROGER PENROSE
12. STAMP
13. FRANCE
14. CHARCOAL
15. MOSAIC MURALS
16. ISRAEL
17. STING
18. ANDRE AGASSI
19. DEAR ABBY
20. PASTEL
21. CASSIUS CLAY
22. COMIC STRIP
23. OSLO ACCORDS
24. SHANGHAI
25. DANCING
26. SAINT LOUIS
27. YOSEMITE
28. DIALOGUE
29. IRONY
30. ORBIT
31. AMERICAN
32. GREEN CARD
33. POLISH POPE
34. NARNIA
35. SEAL
36. ASIAN
37. RADIUM
38. CHESHIRE
39. CANADIAN
40. LE GENERAL
41. LIAR LIAR
42. INDIANA
43. TAIWAN
44. SIMPSONS
45. JETS
46. THE TENTH MAN
47. BONANZA
48. DEAF
49. CAR
50. REPORTER
51. TOOL TIME
52. TENNIS
53. UKRANIAN
54. DYAN CANNON
55. DIARIES
56. FABLES
57. ICE-BORG
58. ETHICS
59. QUE SERA, SERA
60. GILDA RADNER
61. MORTENSON
62. BALLETS
63. SÁRI
64. BART CONNER
65. NIGHT
66. KOREAN
67. H.G. WELLS
68. DISGUISE
69. DARK HORSE
70. OSCAR
71. MADONNA
72. BAUHAUS
73. ERASER
74. SATIRES
75. MYSTERY
76. ERIC BLAIR
77. AIRPORT
78. MAUGHAM
79. ACADEMY
80. ANNIE HALL
81. TEACHER
82. ARCHITECT
83. EAMES
84. SERVANT
85. SURREAL
86. ROBOTICS
87. GELLER
88. MEMORY
89. KANSAS
90. HEBREW
91. BABIES
92. THIN ICE
93. SILENCE
94. MAHATMA
95. CELLO PLAYER
96. ORIOLES
97. ARAB LEADER
98. CHOCOLATE
99. COILS
100. LAWYER

HINTS (occupations)

1. American president
2. American actor
3. American entertainer
4. American musician
5. Burmese diplomat
6. South African president
7. Spanish painter
8. American writer
9. American actress
10. American president
11. Dutch artist
12. American civil rights leader
13. American statesman
14. French painter
15. Russian painter
16. Israeli prime minister
17. American musician and composer
18. German tennis player
19. American advice columnist
20. American painter
21. American boxer
22. American cartoonist
23. Palestinian president
24. Chinese basketball player
25. American actress
26. British poet
27. American photographer
28. Italian astronomer
29. Norwegian playwright
30. Russian cosmonaut
31. American bicyclist
32. French actor
33. Polish religious leader
34. British writer
35. German model
36. Japanese figure skater
37. Polish-French physicist and chemist
38. British writer
39. Canadian prime minister
40. French president
41. Canadian-American actor
42. American basketball player
43. Taiwanese president
44. American tennis player
45. American football player
46. British writer
47. Canadian actor
48. American actress
49. American political activist
50. American vice president
51. American comedian and actor
52. Hungarian-American tennis player
53. Ukranian figure skater
54. American actor
55. French-American writer
56. Greek writer
57. Swedish tennis player
58. Greek philosopher
59. American actress
60. American actor
61. American actress
62. Hungarian composer and pianist
63. Hungarian-American actress

64. Romanian-American gymnast
65. Romanian-American writer
66. South Korean diplomat
67. American actor
68. British actor
69. British rock musician
70. British actor
71. Argentine first lady
72. Swiss painter
73. American actor
74. French writer
75. American writer
76. British writer
77. British rock musician
78. French painter
79. French writer
80. American actor and director
81. Greek philosopher
82. Chinese-American architect
83. Finnish-American architect
84. Dutch painter
85. Spanish artist
86. American writer
87. American actor
88. Spanish painter
89. American basketball player
90. Israeli prime minister
91. American physician
92. Norwegian figure skater
93. French entertainer
94. Indian statesman
95. American musician
96. Dominican baseball player
97. Egyptian president
98. British writer
99. Croatian-American inventor
100. French painter

ABOUT THE AUTHOR

ROY LEBAN has been solving and constructing puzzles most of his life. His puzzles have appeared in *The New York Times*, the *Los Angeles Times*, *Games* magazine, *The Chronicle of Higher Education*, and in newspapers, books, and puzzle collections around the world. He also creates puzzles and puzzle hunts for private and corporate use. He is a member of the National Puzzlers' League, a contributor to several MIT Mystery Hunts, and a cofounder of the Microsoft Puzzle Hunt.

Roy spends his days with puzzles of a different sort—designing and building highly usable computer software, work that's included groundbreaking products in desktop productivity, early tablet computers, and Web publishing. He lives in Redmond, Washington, with his wife, two kids, six computers, three Nikons, and a pizza oven.